The Derelict Daughter

The Derelict Daughter

BRITTNEY SCOTT

newamericanpress
Milwaukee, Wis.

newamericanpress
www.NewAmericanPress.com
© 2018 by Brittney Scott

All rights reserved. No part of this publication may be reproduced, stored in a retrieval system, or transmitted, in any form or by any means, electronic, mechanical, photocopying, recording, or otherwise, without the prior written permission of the copyright holder.

ISBN 978-1-941561-10-2

Book design by David Bowen

Cover image © Ryan Woolgar
https://www.ryanwoolgar.com/

For ordering information, please contact:
Ingram Book Group
One Ingram Blvd.
La Vergne, TN 37086
(800) 937-8000
orders@ingrambook.com

Grateful acknowledgement is made to the editors of the following journals and anthologies in which these works or earlier versions previously appeared:

Alaska Quarterly Review: "I'm Dropping Things I Want to Keep Hidden"; *Arroyo*: "Great Expectations"; *Barrow Street*: "Coming"; *Basalt*: "The Measuring of Time Using Roses, Using Trees" (as "Heirloom"); *Best New Poets 2014*: "The Money Shot"; *Bettering American Poetry 2015*: "Faith in Love and Quantum Physics";

The Boiler: "Points of Entry"; *Cincinnati Review*: "Daughter of Wild Hedges"; *Copper Nickel*: "Signs"; *Cold Mountain Review*: "The Traveler"; *Confrontation*: "Practical Naturalist, Figure 1." (as "Practical Naturalist"), "Resin, Linen, Salt"; *Crab Orchard Review*: "Landfall" (as "On the Edge of Tornado Alley"); *Crosswinds Poetry Journal*: "Things I Did after the Rejection"; Dorothy Sargent Rosenberg Poetry Prize: "Schema," "The Place Where My Dreams Still Happen"; *Event Magazine*: "The Party People"; *Folio*: "After the Service," "What Ran in the Paper"; *The Fourth River*: "On Leaving the Midwest"; *Grist*: "Now Every Man's Arm is Fire"; *Indiana Review*: "Hunger" (as "Not Eating"); *Jabberwock Review*: "What to Expect When You're Expecting"; *The Journal*: "Mystique"; *Cutthroat*, Joy Harjo Poetry Prize: "The Winter Following My Father's Death"; *KNOCK*: "In the Great Green Room," "Letter to Myself in Moments of Misery"; *The Liberal Media Made Me Do It!* (Lummox Press): "My Brother's Wandering Soul"; *Linebreak*: "Faith in Love and Quantum Physics"; *Lake Effect*: "A Sleepwalker's Forecast"; *Meridian*: "Shadow Box"; *Moon City Review*: "The Weight Aurora Carries"; *Narrative Magazine*, 30 Below Contest finalist: "Day Lilies," "Light Pollution"; *The New Guard*, Poetry Contest finalist: "The Weather of Dream"; *The New Republic*: "Why We Bird"; *New South*: "Still Life with Misgivings"; *Notre Dame Review*: "Blue Period," "Even as We Sleep"; *Painted Bride Quarterly*: "Daughter of Wild Lettuce," "After the Hunt"; *Passages North*: "Medium"; *Poet Lore*: "Wearing My Brother's Boxers"; *Prairie Schooner*: "My Brother's Wandering Soul," "Paganism and the Modern Woman"; *Prime Number Magazine*: "To the Teeth"; *Quarter After Eight*: "The Test"; *Quiddity*: "Bright Angel Shale" (as "Bright Angel"); *Qu*: "The Diagnosis"; *The Raleigh Review*: "Schema"; *Salamander*: "Microchimerism"; *Salt Hill*: "The American"; *Slice*: "Scent"; *Slippery Elm*: "Pastoral with Brother"; *Spoon River Poetry Review*: "Nighttime Hymnal"; *Stand Magazine*: "I Do Not Know You"; *Water~Stone Review*: "In the Farthest Fields of Kentucky"

The Derelict Daughter

I
After, After, After

Medium	13
To the Teeth	14
A Sleepwalker's Forecast	17
I'm Dropping Things I Want to Keep Hidden	18
Pastoral with Brother	20
Wearing My Brother's Boxers	21
What Ran in the Paper	24
After the Service	26
Microchimerism	28
Points of Entry	29
Signs	31
The Weight Aurora Carries	33
Faith in Love and Quantum Physics	35
Shadow Box	37
Blue Period	39
Things I Did After the Rejection	41
The Place Where Your Dreams Still Happen	43
Light Pollution	44
Schema	46

II
Unstable Gardener

Daughter of Wild Lettuce	51
Hunger	52
Bloodhound Gang Went Mainstream in 1999	54
Still Life with Misgivings	56

Mystique	57
While I'm Under	58
What to Expect When You're Expecting	59
Day Lilies	61
The Measuring of Time Using Roses, Using Trees	63
Bright Angel Shale	65
Practical Naturalist, Figure 1.	67
The Party People	69
Paganism and the Modern Woman	70
The Weather of Dreams	72
Letter to Myself in Moments of Misery	74
Nighttime Hymnal	76
On Leaving the Midwest	78
The Diagnosis	79
Daughter of Wild Hedges	80
Resin, Linen, Salt	82

III

All Burning

In the Farthest Fields of Kentucky	87
In the Great Green Room	89
Now Every Man's Arm is Fire	90
Great Expectations	91
The Money Shot	92
The Test	93
Why We Bird	94
The American	96
The Traveler	98
I Do Not Know You	100
Scent	101
After the Hunt	103

The Winter Following My Father's Death	104
Even as We Sleep	106
Landfall	107

I

After, After, After

Medium

I've dug up my brother
and propped him against my shoulder,
his weight like a sagged-bag of dog food.
He tells me that he is the vehicle
and the medium, he says now you cannot forget.
His eyes are stale carnations,
jaw unhinged like a life-sized marionette.
And the maggots speak,
they travel in and out of his mouth
like words.

To the Teeth

I was born a brontosaurus sister,
no incisors formed in utero.
A defect, crooked
smile left of the nose, my turtle chin sucking
overbite back into the throat.
It could be I was forgotten,
displaced, in those crucial weeks,
for my already born brother
perfect and insane.

*

Stored in a wooden box
my rotten ectopic teeth,
filled with a painful silver,
smelled like a hollow cave. A constant
rattle to childhood memory,
she'd be so lovely if she fixed her teeth.
At month's end there was no money for the soft-spoken
and I have the furthest thing from fangs.

*

In reoccurring dreams, my palm is a bowl of teeth,
mouth without means to receive
some important message.
A robed woman climbs the hill to my door,
one man pillared at each elbow.
It snows silently all around them.
This has no footprints,
only homecoming and departure.

*

Mouth also means entry,
a doorway to a long velvet hall.
Tusks are elongated incisors,
so necessary for social exchange,
dominance, protection,
tools for digging if nothing else.
I am a sonata played underwater,
the notes float to the surface,
muted and dissonant.

*

On a lover's neck, my bite marks form
an imperfect ring, a gate that allows
the dog out, rabbit in to eat
everything delicious in the garden
so there's nothing left for dinner.

*

Chinese folklore warns of teeth
falling out in dreams,
a foreshadowing of death. That,
or your jaw-deep wisdom
teeth are missing. Mine came in,
room or not, like old plateaus,
and the wind keeps coming, the sun
sets over the colored dust, the sun sets
but nothing's forgotten.

*

Kentucky fields pushed their history skyward,
arrowheads breaking the surface.
My brother and I parted the bluegrass
for gnawed stone, judo, and bodkin points
jabbing through the fleshy soil.

*

Dust coated the exposed nerve
where my front teeth were knocked out,
hit in the mouth by a chain
my brother swirled around him
like fate coming into fruition.
I gummed a spoon of mud. Blood
a collection of circles in the dry dirt,
cells multiplying in the fever.

A Sleepwalker's Forecast

You said it would fall
and crush you, the phantom
chandelier unhinged
from its archaic pulley,
but there was nothing
in the hall that night.
Nothing but air
rising from the rusted iron vent,
fusing our old house in panic
as if we left the stove scalding,
as if you slept among embers.
Mom had you by the shoulders,
her long nightgown brushing the floor
as she tried to steer you back
to bed. Your eyes, not blinking, rose
to something we couldn't see.
Sweat covered your forehead.
She didn't listen
to what you were saying, mouth moving,
arms over your head to block the fallout.
I was there at the edge
of my room, in a shirt of yours
I'd grow into
without you.

I'm Dropping Things I Want to Keep Hidden

A split branch broke
through our window last night,
slicing my brother's head
clean from his body.
All day, I tell this story to my second-grade classmates
until it is as true as that windy night—

True as the elm in my front yard
with branches that eat at the siding,
true as the two floor-to-ceiling windows
with mammoth glowing curtains
that puff in the moonlight like giant jellyfish.

These are facts.
Someone tells the teacher,
not because he is dead, but because I am lying.
My brother is three years ahead of me,
down the hall, checking his spelling
while news spreads of his death.

I am confronted about this lie in the red playhouse
behind our cubbies.
The teacher sits in a small chair shaped like a bear
ready to grip.
Confronted by a grown woman being mauled by a bear,
she asks if I am confused or mistaken.
She asks if bad dreams

misplace reality.
It hurts to put it back together the right way.

There is a naked Barbie in my backpack,
which is in my cubby, and I am embarrassed that she is listening.

I want my brother's head to vanish,
rain to mold the carpet into map lichen.
I want to wake
in the forest with walking sticks and a headless shaman
who leads me to a valley

instead of grinding his boot into my back,
instead of locking me in the root cellar for two days.
I'm dropping things I want to keep hidden
down the holes he's punched in the walls.

By lunch some girl will lean close to his ear
and say, "I heard you died, I heard you
died before the sun came up."
And for the rest of the day his letters will glow
off the woody page. With his pencil

at the peak of its sharpness,
he will pause for once
before pressing too hard,
before breaking the lead and losing the word.

Pastoral with Brother

They found you thrashing
in a field of crab grass,
a windmill of boy
limbs pumping the air, the dirt,

the grasshoppers leaping
up and out
of your way.

They knew you
by your swerving silhouette
staining the bucolic sunset,
the wide open spaces,

with your bright red,
vomit-stained jersey,
your rat tail hanging
out of your backwards hat.

You punched two cops
before they used their boots
to press your cheek
flushed with whiskey

into the thistle, rubbing
mouth and jaw raw,
until you couldn't speak.

Wearing My Brother's Boxers

because I am both siblings—
the derelict daughter waist high in water,
looking at her reflection
when it should be the brother

underneath. I am the brother below
my still-shy hips and bulbous knees,
wearing his race-car boxers, wearing

another face.
I can't tell anymore
if they're cars or streaks of tar
blackening the fissured track,
a circle winding

my waist, the tag still carrying
a faded inmate number
from the years he wasted in juvie.
I never saw him

wear these boxers
so now the memory is anything
inside my body. I went to visit when I was twelve,
three years younger than he was then,
fifteen years older now,

an impossible math.
I've blamed the watch
he pilfered from somebody's wrist
much larger than his own.

*

Another thing we shared,
delicate bone structure, a frame only half
built. His hands were very clean.
While I was there, someone bent down
and shit in the corner, a believable color
against whitewash gray.

Inside, he earned his G.E.D.,
got beaten with a metal lunch tray,
he lost weight and grew tall.
I've grown in and out,

but his body's lingering smell ached
when we cleared the closet
as if his clothes could only
hold him if they held on together.

It feels like he came directly home
and unpacked the gun,
nuzzling it against his temple,
a love that blasted us open.

Really it was four years later
when he stole the gun
from his friend's crazy mom
who stored weapons and water
in case of apocalypse.

But it was my brother
who climbed through her basement window,
and it was his life,
not the world, that would end.

*

When I was small, my head
barely to his chest, heartbeat
closer than his voice or bad breath,
he used to trap me under the hamper,
a little laundry prison.

He would offer his hands
through the basket's holes
for me to hold until I stopped crying,
as if he wanted to apologize
but he wasn't about to let me go.

What Ran in the Paper

It looks like something is in your mouth, one last supper or the bullet you're finally ready to spit out. *Christopher Allen Scott, 18. The cause of death is under investigation. He was employed as an engine disassembler*, which means he took things apart, which means he was always dirty. Blue collar, no farther than the sixth grade, a G.E.D. class in juvie. *Surviving are his mother*, but barely, *his father*, for another three months exactly. His body will lie in the same hospital room as his son's. Bone of his bone, flesh of his flesh. *And a sister*, me. He tried to shoot me first; I like to think this is because he loved me most, loved me more than he loved himself. If you come over the bullet still dines in the kitchen linoleum. He was not a solid shot, that's why he placed the gun so very close to his face. *Service will be held in the morning*; it wasn't even midnight, the moon a pale yawn. *The Rev. James T. Heady officiating.* Who is my brother's representative? We have never been baptized or christened and the only body he ever took was his own. *With a burial in Oak Hill Cemetery.* He is not resting on a hill, and few trees are oak, nothing the way you picture, nothing covered with a canopy's deep reprieve.

He is buried, restlessly, by a lost field's edge, abandoned to brown bottles. *Friends may call*, no matter how stunned they are into silence. *Friends may call* but they won't.

After the Service

Like umbrellas over an ocean, this fungus
found in Michigan, two one thousands old,
covers forty acres underground.
The fleshy tunnels,

a safety-net beneath
the countryside,   the cooking show clean up,
pulsing the dying
vomit verdant.
What is unseen
takes us under. Without, our dead
pile over.   Without, who would gate-keep
the threshold between living and   , who
                            would soak
us into meal? I have eaten

my father. I eat my brother bitterly.
We are living rot; my mother's bedpan, a sun tea, soaks
on the lawn, hidden between
ugly heirloom tomatoes—
purple fatty folds unfurled and eaten off the vine.
The juice drips past my belly

button. Inky caps
bloom inky in the non-hours,
then dissolve themselves
                          into puddles of blackish stink.
Nightsoil parasol—
what they contain instead of calories,
non-sexed for the sun, prodigious
                          milks of lunar energy.

*

Under old oaks, reprieve. We go to snack
and mourn. I've thrown the cheese tray into the creek—
it floats like a dead possum, teats up.
It is impossible to predict

when and where

the next mushrooms will flaunt and gloat.
                    We know after the rain.
We know it happens at night. In the basement,
refreshments will be served following the ceremony.

Microchimerism

> *The living cells of her fetus persist in a mother after giving birth.*
> —Michael Verneris

Your dying burnt the wires to the house,
left you oscillating in our mother

like a cracked heliograph in shade.
I kiss her open-mouthed,

a call to you thrown down
this bottomless well, panic not hearing

sound come back. Moss stops growing half way,
circles some unreachable brink.

At the town's farthest edge,
the ladder rusted off the water tower.

You are locked
in the root cellar, in the grainless silo

at the back of our property.
I wait for you to send word

from the room in which you were built,
the last room in which you are still living.

Points of Entry

There is always the shower,
flailing face-first, a brief dance before
your teeth burst loose, neck snapping
lights-out style. The water descends,

it darkens around you.
Think about sockets, those friendly faces
grinning up from the baseboards.
All it takes is one wire's wrongful rub

against another. A meeting between you
and a yard-sale toaster warm under the weekend sun.
Is your basement dirt based?
Radon rises through your floor's imperfections,

infests your body, enters
undetectable like the holy ghost, happiness,
those dreams you have of falling.
Bed linens are woven with formaldehyde,

a carcinogen which eventually fills you fully—
your lusty breakdown's only preservative.
It's coming, and you're already floating off.
Your soft cavities will soften,
blood will clot against you.
The hoary oak drops its legacy

on the roof nightly, the damage it does
to silence, to forgetfulness,
your long-standing denial
that unless you take an ax into its thick ringed trunk,

*

it will be here after you—the whole block,
fever, toxic plants, your pill bottles
expiring. All of it goes on without you.

Signs

Forsythia goes mustard with early May across the yard
and he dies again. He dies

as often as day lilies. But the wound,
creeping Charlie, wanders

around my brother's body.
The creek behind our house chokes

waiting for rain. A delicate algae
films over. My mind films over—

I cover the hole in his temple
with a starfish. His guts slip

with the freshwater eels. Velvet ants, dried blood,
disperse. I dream of him, a nightmare root deep

under a black willow. I feel responsible
for the creek, haul buckets from the pump

to drown my reflection. Underneath,
invisible currents circulate.

This sun, the one that rose
the morning after, after, after needs

something dark to shine on.
He shot himself while I was lying down

*

in the next room. Sound
bigger than sound. Someone

left an oak door under his old window.
I don't know how

it happened exactly, so it happens
over and over. Wind,

on its way through the bamboo
by the water, says, *Shh Shh*, the tupelo says, *Shh Shh*.

The Weight Aurora Carries

It splits me open knowing
I couldn't pull him

from his violent burning.
How the world spun in fury

to me, as if I were responsible
for letting my brother die.

And how my sister's face eclipsed
upon knowing her favorite sibling,

who always brought the perfect gift
wrapped in carbon paper,

was lost. In this new eternal dark
there is nowhere to travel.

Now my mother tilts
to no one; her life buckles

under the starry cloak.
But I was the one

who heaved herself over
the horizon to retrieve him.

I was the one that made him rise
after night's long ruin.

*

Couldn't anyone see me? I was there,
I was standing just in front of him.

Faith in Love and Quantum Physics

In one, my brother's in the gutter,
literally, face up almost floating along

2nd street after a hard rain, the clouds
finally clearing, the clean stars directing

traffic, his indelibly dirty palm planted
around a forty, which, in this life,

is all he ever drank.
In another, my brother isn't wrecked.

He owns a headshop in California's forgiving coast.
He has a beard, the tattoo of his nickname

retouched to add a vine of morning glories
for his wife, Glory, who watches home movies

of when he, we, were kids. What's important
is that he isn't dead in all of them. String Theory

suggests there are unlimited universes
exploding every second on top of each other,

each one different, a single action reversed,
rearranged, vastly, to slightly different.

He still dies in some, in many, but so do I.
He shoots me and then himself,

*

and we both disperse, keep running
in so many other directions that it doesn't matter

how bad it hurts. He's just an asshole
most of the time. I've even stopped talking to him,

cut off all communication after he stole my car,
stole my wedding ring for heroin,

whatever he's done. I have no brother,
I say to my friends at dinner parties.

Which is a privilege given
only to those who have them to disown.

I straighten my high-collared dress,
think of him out there, somewhere,

anywhere but where this life keeps him now.
I stare out the window at my face half-hidden,

half-reflected in the glass and the shifting ring of light
left on at the end of the walk.

Shadow Box

Upon unearthing the ability
to reverse extinction, pulling
deep genetic root from loam,

they plan to restore
the ivory-billed woodpecker
to pine forests, to swampland,

to haunts that surrendered his perch,
thinking we can take it all
back as long as the spiral burns.

*

And does that mean, long-dead brother,
they can pluck from me a strand
of hair familiar enough to helix

and birth you again?
Switch on the headlamp,
the dust brush hits like a pickaxe in the dark.

Death sieved clean, loose and ephemeral as dirt
shaken from a map. When you separate
from me you'll only look the part,

the way no one will
care when the ivory-bill is just a flameback
disguised in a red cap.

*

I just need to know he's there,
in a fir tree's decaying burl, poised
like a clay-fired figurine

perfectly rendered from life.
Yet, by the turbid water, still,
the ivory-bill's distinct call,

said to have echoed like a toy trumpet,
will be absent. With this new, unfamiliar voice,
he doesn't know that song, doesn't even know how to sing.

Blue Period

Someone left a balled-up child's sock,
all lonely looking
in the washer, abandoned at the laundromat.

I plan for the future:

tonight I'll warm up a Banquet
dinner in the microwave
and the moths will forget the moon for the fat
bare bulb of porch light.

There is an onion rolling around in my head.

My brother shot himself fifteen years ago today, each day
shot by something.

If I stick my head in a dryer it sounds like a womb. A bullet hole

in the glass door rises into vision like a sun spot,
a picture flashed without asking.

Someone painted a blue sky
on the empty wall above the dryers
with sundresses and bloomers puffing in the pretend breeze.
Even a stuffed bear lovingly hangs on the line.

Butterflies and bluebirds.

It's like one of those dreams where you run toward someone you love
who is in danger, who has been hurt,

*

the person you love has been hurt badly,

but the ground just keeps coming up under your feet
and the only embrace you'll be granted
is the ever-expanding distance between.

Things I Did after the Rejection

I went to the library downtown
with its eight gray Corinthian columns.
City sounds banged around in the entryway—
the honking and the roadwork,
the drunk who's always on the steps,
plastic bags rubber-banded over his shoes,
or no shoes, I'm not certain.
He's yelling the word, *Godzilla!*
Godzilla! Gooooodzilla!
I didn't want to go,
and I felt like having a private pitiful cry.
I wore black combat boots
and incredibly saggy leggings.
I had forgotten my coat and was baptized
among the early February ghosts,
my least favorite month.

And you would think all those books would mock me
with their success
like clamoring tropical parakeets,
but they didn't.
The long warm rows were such a comfort.
No one bothered me;
The information desk was empty
but for three delicate deer-foot ferns
sending their fuzzy feelers over
the porcelain rim of their pots.
A rough-looking boy in an oversized Raiders coat,
just the way my brother used to look
before he shot himself, that old story

I never shut up about,
had books laid out on a smooth pine table.
While reading, he gently rested his cheek on a novel's
worn manila page.
The other books circled
his head like friendly angels.
He looked as if he might drift off before finishing the page.
I walked past him, farther into the stacks
where the lights laid a dim route before me
and I began to feel a bit better.

The Place Where Your Dreams Still Happen

In your last living minute,
after sending a bullet
through your temple
to lodge below your shell-shaped ear—
you are five again,
chasing the Ohio River's curve,
free from our mother's clasping hand.
Two pennies, two pebbles,
and a brass key slap against your thigh.
Overwhelmed, pockets heavy,
you tip into the swelling
blue water. The sun dives
into the horizon. The end
of a long cloudless day.

Light Pollution

We are a million years homeless,
maybe more, maybe closer
to when we burned

our first body, some soul's charred bones
collapsed back in a damp cave.
The first twig's fevered snap,

a branded smell, not like fear, not like silent joy,
more like power opening a gold halo
around us. This is the moment we decided

we were owed. And then we started killing
whales, their fat molded and blazed,
propped in brass chandeliers which hung above us,

a moth's misguiding moon.
Our time marked as decreasing,
each candle lined with weight,

a note dropped hourly, forsaking
our dark heart's circular pulse.
There was no need to ever look up again.

Edison's incandescent mistake,
filament by filament,
blazed up in pupil-shrinking exactness.

We are actually letting less and less in.
We forget the depth-dancing optic strain
of nights pitched an honest dark.

*

With each porch light left bright,
the stars, those distant watchers,
grow dimmer, retreating farther and farther

back into our past. All this time, all this
long while, even in Sutherland's safest bend,
we sway, one by one,

away from lightless sight. We forget
dead reckoning, the way we once grew to trust
the space in front of us, to follow

the hunter and his faithful dog
who still keeps the brightest star like a beacon
wedged in the pocket of his mouth.

Schema

> *The wound is the place where the Light enters you.*
> —Rumi

I live inside my brother's death
    inside his angry wound
                    He rode through the wooden door
to the room with the darkness
    It was fall, early dark
when he shot himself
              The sound of his body dropping
was the new moon's invisible rise
was my body
        waking from a long sleep
in the darkness

I lived in the room
until my brother shot a hole through his head
        he shot light through the ceiling

Now I live inside
my brother's thumb-shaped tunnel

Acorns fell where his body dreamed
                      Thick ringed trees grew whole
from the hole below his ear, the place I climbed from
                          and up
                          and up

I am awake inside the space he left
I make the shape
of my brother's white body   I fill the space my brother would fill

*

His blood was light's first pinhole
shot through the night sky
                      They grew and burned and made people
and dogs, houses, fish,
rooms with darkness
            light in them
votives I can follow with my body
                  my body holds the shape of grace

II

Unstable Gardener

Daughter of Wild Lettuce

My mother plants snow peas behind the garage.
She works around the sink hole that takes
dry leaves and garbage all summer.

In her memory, I am an almost abortion.
She plants marigolds with the tomatoes,
symbiotic bright suns

bursting between the rows.
Sometimes she knows, love
abounding, sometimes she overlooks

an entire season's glut, and rot
carries us through winter.
In the cellar, plastic roses, night crawlers,

unfinished half-hearted projects,
the potatoes' all seeing eyes and me
damp through my nightshirt.

No natural light filters in,
so I only know the earth's eternal hour.

My mother, an unstable gardener,
tosses spare seeds into barren patches
of the backyard. We won't know until spring.

Sometimes new buds shoot up
in the most unusual places,
but more often, they don't.

Hunger

A halo of bone-hollow
dryness, the way the atmosphere lifts
even after a day or two.

I feel like a desiccated gourd,
                          my body,
                          my viscera like a woman's

open hair clip, only the bursting
                                ribbed claw.

I am the sound your lips make, pushing air
through the thinnest
reed or dry rush,

thistle with all the white, milky
                          slough pulled out,

the inner poisonous stalk,
the part you may touch, but never indulge in.
When I'm lying on my stomach, it appears
                                      as if parts have vanished,
my torso, the entire area,
                    gone, and I am floating

just above the bed, a mere cloud full of dreams.

This strange sensation—this moment when the pieces that will
        always be
with me, until I am not what I am, are gone—feels like relief.

*

I have the power
to put it there, to take it away and
bring it back, the nameless thing keeping me
                                              tethered.

The only way is to keep from it

all that it begs for.
        It begs and you pour it out.

It asks and you respond with silence,
                and the silence builds an echo inside yourself,
                                              inside all the

        hollow walls
which have been washed clean. Tell me,

what you would do
with an endless hunger. If you have tried
        to please it, you know
it can never be pleased.

If you have given it what it asks for you know
                        it only asks for more.

Bloodhound Gang Went Mainstream in 1999

My first girlfriend kept her mattress in a small walk-in closet. In the morning I woke in closet-darkness, slamming my head against the low sloped ceiling. I was fourteen and we were both very bad spellers. I was trying to be a writer and a vegetarian. No one delivered pizza to her neighborhood and the entire block smelled like fire when it rained. Next door, the house was badly burned; only one loadbearing wall stood erect. Sometimes we played strip poker with her friends, who were no one's friends, strangers, which made it easy to take off my clothes. The same Bloodhound Gang track would play on repeat. We sat in a circle and time spun around the card table, and I lived the same ten minutes drunk and shirtless. *The roof, the roof, the roof is on fire.* At night, after an hour of clumsy sex, she told me stories while stroking the sweaty underside of my breast, the left one, which is bigger, which looks more like a pale velvet moon. This was the story, which she swore was true, of the scorched neighbor's house:

The man who lived there caught mice and burned them alive in his backyard leaf pile. He kicked his wife in the stomach when she didn't change the air filters enough. The man carried them, the mice, by the tails and tossed them into the licking flames of the fire. He stood in heavy boots, leaning against the doorjamb, some deep satisfaction watching a small animal burn. But eventually one of the mice escaped, leaves fusing to his grey soiled fur, already blind and depthless, and he ran straight up the steps, right under the man's wide stance and into his house, into his sad wife's drapes dyed with onion skin and burned the entire place down.

She was not exactly a good kisser, but she looked like the girl I loved deeply from a distance. I can only guess who I was standing in for, what hole I was filling. Or worse, I was the girl she loved deeply. She got me a job in a food court, Chix and Edie Peppers, which was half fried chicken stand, half Mexican restaurant. We worked both sides. We rode the bus to work. The first time riding a bus I threw up in the driver's waste bin. We took tacos home at night. I gave up being a vegetarian. My mother slept with a redhead named Marvin who sold her drugs so we didn't stay at my house. We used to walk to the elementary school park to push each other in the swings, but stopped because some sow-bellied man in a garage apartment kept kneeling in front of his door and jerking off. He came on the glass storm door. His cum, even from a distance, was cloudy. He had wild dogs chained to his steps. Sometime after she and I broke up, the man was found dead in the back of his house, hunched over a half painted blue dragon figurine. Like most colors, blue doesn't really exist; it is more of a reflection of absence. Absence is the only real color.

Still Life with Misgivings

At the sink, a homely composition:
black-handled ladle,
wire-domed whisk,
a blue plate's perfect arch.

My mother runs water over bowls
ringed with last night's dinner.
Grease pools color,
rubbed from the steel pots.

Kitchenware shipwrecked
on her shore nightly and fog-ridden.
She hears her small voice asking
permission, the Brillo pad, the wedding

glass's fragile silver rim.
Blown-out roses
turn potpourri on the table.
She raises a wine flute

from the sink, still wet,
and holds it to the west.
The lip burns red, caught
in the mouth of the sun.

Mystique

They could smell me, ready to pound them
                                 with my iron anvil, my pad
like a pungent sidekick.
I started my period and ducks caught in the mud, a brown bouquet
         of toilet paper was hung in all the windows.
Our insides are falling
               out in the worst array
                              of colors. All the business of moons,
new and full, and us
unable to receive the communion wafer.   Mouth opening to flesh, fear
coating the ribs like hickory smoke—
you can't know the source.

I went to the social and rode the Ferris wheel until they turned off
        the lights.
It looked different
         from the top, games
                      shadowed and distant, the goldfish
certain to float.
            Contestants jerked their sights
away from the wooden bulls-eyed ducks,
to the doves
      on the wire, took aim
and shot. They burst like puffs of milkweed slough.

Blood is under the nails, in all the purple creases.
                             I squat down, knees bulbous as onions,
      and burn the hair off.
I do not like chocolate or soaps.
A hard crust cakes the edges.

While I'm Under

I remove my underwear and dress
in paper, a sound like chewing
when I lie back. The doctor prods
my womb like sounding a lake.
I hold my body

like a basin.
I dream of fruit
in the kitchen back home:
apple, pomegranate, plum, missing
seeds and stars. Hollowed
sound of growth, a bloom
heavy inside, a cracking
somewhere deep.
How vacant it feels, solitary
in the sterile silver bowl
which tips them
so easily out.

What to Expect When You're Expecting

I called her my daughter,
carried her against my hip, always.
Each morning I braided her horse hair
with a silver comb. Her glass eyes shut
when I laid her down. We slept.

I forgot her by the water
while it rained all night.
In the morning I found her sunken
in mud, a centipede hooked like jewelry
around her neck.

*

There is jabber for women
who wish to speak it—the way we favor
the mandrake's human shape.
Suggestive rarity digs its heels
deeper in the dirt, suckles the sticky
white liquid and grows a radicle.
Uva-ursi rubs the jack pine raw,
returns the womb to normal size

after birth. The flowers sag
like pellucid-pink bells, a veined
and delicate throbbing. Choked
freesia overrun with poke.
And it's berberis, motherwort,
feverfew, and bitter rue
blooming yellow with regret.

*

Bury it and it won't come back.
Eat it and it was never not you.
The afterbirth is more the fetus's
friend than the mother. A porous
thieving that protects
you from yourself.

Day Lilies

You are an heiress to a feral cat colony,
a trailer collapsing into a faulty foundation,
suicide letters, aluminum pipes, brass wiring
which promises the lights will burn out,
and your mother will eventually die.
Your memory tells you that most things you try to save

cannot be saved.
She used to feed a family of groundhogs
on the edge of your backyard's gentle slope,
where you planted orange day lilies.

They are called that, day lilies,
because they see the sun run its solitary line
once. Only once.
But it's ok; it's not as bad as you think.

See there—
on the tepid green stalks
is another, and another, an entire bushel waiting
patiently for the day to wear them out.
She used to feed the family of groundhogs;
your mother put out food and watched from the kitchen window.
The curtains were stained yellow,

in the way you are stained with this recollection
of someone who cared about you deeply
who doesn't anymore. She won't get out of bed;
you try to call her, just now,
but she doesn't pick up.

*

You picture a row of large gray birds weighing the phone lines,
the phone itself gray under dust's tender sheet.
She's not even a violent drinker,
can't get drunk with fervor. She buys Coors Light,
dutifully, with caution,
and drinks one right after another
until she passes out with the TV's sad blue light.

The last time she visited she didn't eat
for two days. She only eats condiments,
pickles, slices of cheap sharp cheddar,
hot dogs warmed in the microwave. Your mother,
she tells you it isn't her,
she's sick, her age has fallen over her like a decaying log,
but my god, nothing keeps her from drinking.
Nothing stops

her from thoughtfully putting the cans upside down in the sink
so all night they keep you up,
draining. You
think about the groundhogs, their hunger
and bewilderment as they paw the empty table.

In the morning they are empty.
They are hollow and soundless.
On the rare occasion she buys glass bottles
she will whistle over the lip,
a note you remember from early childhood.

The sound will deepen as she drinks.
It will deepen and grow richer
and then there will be no sound at all.

The Measuring of Time Using Roses, Using Trees

There are heirloom roses cut
each morning for the newlyweds,
pungent showy ornaments,

vulgar the way they bare themselves.
I am married to my mother's dying.

In our shared bed, dream's dormant body
tosses between us. A mile from this lodging, down
a path only visible at low tide,

the Klamath River cedes to ocean.
For every morning we stay, fallen
petals ring the living.

Here, in old growth's ledger,
fog and redwood record our burden by expanding.

We follow the lightning-struck trail,
lunette trees burned out in the middle,
my mother dissolves into the trunk's scorched arch.

We watch cormorants buoy and vanish
on the river, stunned each time
their slender necks break

water. Because what are we if not
each other's proof? Sea glass dredges whole

in my dreams, a bottle back together,

knocking against the rocks.
The inn's open windows are like shells we press

our ears to. We can hear
the ocean out there, tearing down the edges,

broadening the river,
its mouth opening wider and wider.

Bright Angel Shale

In electric dusk, the Painted Desert
dissolves into another day's dust.
My mother prepares behind a heavy green curtain,
but no one has seen these canyons

the way John Powell first saw the bright angel
shale and called the layers *leaves*
in a great story book.
Now we are just dry mouths

gaping skyward, the junk-shop burning
tin and plastic above the western rim.
We climb a watchtower
built in place of a watchtower

the Hopi built for ritual.
The gift store is load bearing and expensive.
Far below us, by the curved Colorado
river bottom, where the future dutifully carves

its name, the infantile light brings little money.
Yucca bloom like candles, keeping the moths up
and to their desperations.
Carried by uncharted winds, a condor

descends above our heads like the desert's tumbling
dark. There are no poles down
to the Kiva, no sacred moments, just dirt
dredged between us. Dirt and a camera

cramped with snapshots, raised to the risen
moon's maria—vending machines, deer,
the canyon's neon flickering out.
My mother's eyes are closed.

Practical Naturalist, Figure 1.

Griseous city living corrupts my gentle disposition. Harder still
as the city girdles the domesticated
trees in wire. These trees, they surrender
their holes to rot.

I want to be away from what does and does not
fit b/c high fashion upsets me so much.
Need Supply Co. sells
suspendered black dresses
with hot buttoned hunger. Starved red buttons,
hip-nipping mutts
feasting on what's dumpster thrown,
plate left, mouth kept.
A matte-finished woman wore my black dress
and I clawed her feet for mercy.
Please, God, I said, *please take off that figure.*

There are fitness palaces ringed with exotic shrubs,
pictures of hard work, freedom, black-out
rooms so you can't see where you're not
going. Free pizza every third Tuesday.

In the city my nails need to grow
faster better stronger. My hair lacks flight.
Botticelli's *Birth of Venus* disgusts and shames me.
Not b/c one breast bears witness but b/c her stomach
is so fat and shapeless.
Larger parks, places where we recreate,
harbor hundreds of bored avian species
drained of florescence.

*

When in the wide green open,
you know, yonder, nothing is ill fitted,
nothing pauses above a lake's unmarred sheen.
Flocks plummet and dance
insanely for one another, entire elm forests lie down to mulch.
Out there, the party winds down without a fight.

The Party People

At these parties the people,
the party people
aren't getting older,
and I'm standing around them adding
the years to my stomach,
and pretty soon I'll have to take
their young wet mouths,
open for anything,
and hold them up to the full moon
of my breast beginning to wane
into a half-closed eye
and offer myself as sacrifice
for all the time I've wasted
trying to get them to love me.

Paganism and the Modern Woman

After I gave up the bright sundresses and the jeans,
bananas, and questions, and the silk,
I put away the books
and stood in a gray pinafore at the fence's edge.

I used to be a noisy vehicle.

I was   , the absent
unknowable before.

All it takes is a blackout   for our contours to beat the skin's
lazy drum. I am inside
            and inside the field
piled with hay.

In the dark, the blades of wheat are sharp.
I am the gray pinafore and the old face.

A house appears, the reoccurring house
            from the reoccurring
dirt-forged dream, at the top of a hill,
overlooking the valley's heart.

The hill overlooks my heart. I climb
a ladder to the roof carpeted
with giant primeval ferns. The fronds unfurl the wettest purple
underside.

I crawl to the edge
and look over—

Never this far before,
never past the fasting phosphor horizon,
past the last Venus, the last Vishnu and the tree's sad story,
past the entire rusted day
until I become myself looking at myself
        looking over the edge at myself
standing in a grey pinafore at the fence's edge.

The Weather of Dreams

The air is thin the higher my small dreams float,
tied to a barometer which plunges farther
despite mild weather. The pressure pulls
my sheets into tornadic knots.
I am frightened of what's in me

and what's not. Sometimes I am shot,
thrown from plate-glass windows.
I lean out of broken windows
and see my fallen body,
blood-framed,

one arm raised in question.
My old dog—who had a stroke while I slept,
the previous night's granular clouds of coke
still floating around in my head—
he came and licked my fatal wounds.

Often I am already dead, the dying already over,
and I can never leave. I'm tied to my mother's waist
with red twine. I float around her head, a balloon
blown too full. She is a child tugging

against the air.
It's raining and I'm having sex
on the darkened basalt steps of a temple
with someone I don't know from behind.
My hands and knees chafing through to the bone,

*

my bones knocking at the wet temple door.
Or in the produce section, on a fruit stand after closing.
A flood light's romantic invitation filters in,
but the pomelo's soft glow can't be trusted,
It's all rind. The avocados are overripe.
There is a sense of waiting in the off hours
between open and close, like I only exist as a reflection
of service.

I am breaking up and getting back together
with people I don't love anymore.
My dismembered body dances around a dried well.
I am making mistakes and watching myself ruin a good dress.
Thick fog hovers at eye level.
A mist falls from somewhere.

Letter to Myself in Moments of Misery

I'm dying in my dreams again. The moon crashing behind the house,
tidal waves and tin foil diseases,

like Alzheimer's, b/c they could be linked, you can't trust doctors to
save you. Sometimes I watch myself

die by gun-shot wound, apocalypse, being thrown
twenty-six stories.

I suffer from unspecific anxiety, a little agoraphobia.
People assume this means I am afraid

of open spaces or crowds, and I am, but it's not
what you think.

It's fear of panic in places you can't escape
peacefully

so you can vomit in amity, like nights
spent splayed on the cool bathroom floor,

forehead sweating up the porcelain toilet seat.

If something bad happens somewhere, like childhood,
like the entire state of Indiana, then I will not go back.

Jim Henson, creator of the Muppets, childhood joy, died
from the flesh eating bacteria,

died from something called *necrotizing fasciitis*.

*

Brains seize. Bodies stroke out.
Sometimes it's hard to fall asleep.

Some man or woman that is not me is willing
to have anal sex with my partner, eat steak,

do a throat-closing line of coke.

I am troubled by pandemics and parabens,
dark matter and failure. Revision. Right now,

this right now and your right now,
I am feeling anxious and slightly nauseous.

I am spotting. Sometimes lying in the dark helps.
Sounds, like close

cognates, breathing, *Sh*, and *T*

calm the inside vultures, the maybe cancers.
The fact that you're reading this calms me.

Nighttime Hymnal

On the nights I can't sleep
and the room's corners are wet creases,

I hum the drowsy notes from the nighttime hymnal.
Floating in the dark's rich yolk

are the choruses of the sleepless
and the sun's leftover static, leaping.

I'm somnolent but musical
with the moon's lazy arch falling

past my window.
There is a dense siren in the distance,

on its arch too, in a way,
as it boomerangs closer, then farther away.

There are porch lights and crickets,
and water darkening ditches,

the empty rhythm of vacant park benches.
Someone walks down the graveled alley,

alone with the owl's impossible melody.
Behind the house, the train's humble solo

like your own body's notes
loading its meager cargo.

*

It carries you through
an echoing tunnel,

onto the other side,
which is tomorrow.

On Leaving the Midwest

We see relief leveled and lazy,
stratified as stained glass strung
in the west kitchen bay at sunset,

sunset close as dandelions
in the side yard. We miss every entrance
for the previous. The magic eye

gathers dust, 3D glasses red, red.
The studio bottles, blown and frosted,
ferment in the lens,

empty open like a tunnel's dark.
And still life is not foreground
nor midground, just depth ironed quiet.

This glaze makes us want to blink.
It makes us want to turn
the TV way up. The way

stars span, that flat and tinging
stellar distance, is how we hack the depth
from any voyage or homecoming.

They never leave the periphery,
that vast rim of top hat,
and while they look at the empty hand,

they miss the bright searing colors,
the flash while I tumble over
and parade out of sight.

The Diagnosis

From the winter's blue dark, the crows
floated in through the open window

where my mother and I slept in our shared bed.
They came and burrowed under the quilts,

one on my chest, embracing my heart.
My mother lay motionless. She did not cry

and in the blackness I strained to speak
but my breath froze in the glacial air.

I tried slipping out from beneath the cobalt weight,
as if this burden were a baby

nursing until desiccation.
Corvus lay atop me. Iridescent claws

clasped my sternum, tightened their hold.
Her shadowy feathers only ruffled in reposition

like a mother nesting on top of her clutch,
assiduous and definite,

until something fragile finally escapes.

Daughter of Wild Hedges

My mother is smoke and yellow,
streaked with cave-blue veins.
My mother refuses to shower or bathe.
She soils herself, even though she tries
wobbling to the bathroom, but her body won't
allow forgiveness.
One of her rooms has collapsed into the house's foundation.
Stink flies up from all the closets,
a festering phoenix that should never have risen.
The walls are sallow and wan,
coated with cat hair, bad air, and insect casings.
Roaches gather around the crusted cat shit on the carpet
like desert beasts circling a watering hole.
She stands in front of the walls and disappears,
which is really what she has always wanted.
She will not leave the house unless she has to,
She will not leave
even if I beg. I beg.
She hasn't done laundry in almost a year.
The floor is so black around her bed,
it is as if a million spiders praise her.
She keeps the blinds shut,
and the hedges have grown wild,
blocking all the windows.
She sits cross-legged on the bed like a crumbling Buddha
and rocks back and forth on her brown bare mattress,
all the delicate floral rubbed off from the rocking.
This insignificant square space is the raft that carries
her from one day into the next.

The house sinks into the dirt,
the ceiling is falling,
the sky is falling, the raft is barely afloat.

Resin, Linen, Salt

Driving home, coast-to-coast A.M is just switching to static.
Dawn, glaucous, lays its wet face across the highway.

The host leaves with a story— a mummy,
gently wrapped and preserved

over 10,000 years ago abruptly rose
and strolled across a room before collapsing,

cloth like a coat of trailing ribbon.
Love is strange that way.

*

Before I moved, leapt halfway across country.
My mother tried killing herself four times,

wrote four separate letters
I've hidden in a red box under the bed.

What she calls dust bunnies have gathered
around this burnt red coffin.

One I can read, in the other's her hand slipped
too much, moved right off the page,

pen marks on the linens for so long
after— P, L, Y's illegible question.

*

A leaf that's been stuck
from the start, slapping its little palm

against the windshield, escapes—
a tumble and spiral backwards, away.

Along the highway, shadows of familiar Midwestern trees
fall around each other, darkening the forest floor.

When I get there we hug, her back thin
enough to feel her spine's fragile length, the wells

like hand-grips. She has uncoiled gray,
got dentures, shed weight since I saw her last.

I don't remember who my mother was before
this unhappiness, who she was before

this moment, or how we arrived. Tell me,
how do you preserve what is already gone?

III

All Burning

In the Farthest Fields of Kentucky

Liberty Auto Salvage dishonored my father,
fired him in public for stealing hood ornaments from cars he'd never
touch unwrecked. They burned his last paycheck as penance
for pretending, even in his shed's darkest corner,
he held sway over Mercedes and her soaring angel.

Or this is the story he spills,
after lying me out of school
to cuss the weeded Kentucky fields with him.
I punch the air with right hooks, bob and weave
like the words bob and weave sound
shuffling from a fifth grader's mouth,
and tell my drunk of a father I will kill
for him and his esteem. Whom else

but him, my flagged father woozy with a fifth
of Dark Eyes? We rest along a great and busted
forest's border. Birds from the woods
fly into the field's open mouth. I am hungry
because lunch would be winding down by now,

study hall like a dreamless nap before me.
And it's strange feeling unsafe at moments
when you know safety should swaddle you
with surety. My father's a homicidal rain shadow
painting the horizon black.

In science class I learned that we can detect
lightning's subtle magnetic shifts before the scorching
ground heaves up the flowering sky.

He pulls a gun from his many-pocketed vest.
All around my father, sensitive brier fold their leaves.

Too many targets and the aim of a festering
blame and too many weapons. He stumbles and shoots,
knocking me sideways where I huddled beside him.
Fear and the fired gun make me think I'm bleeding,
but I just landed where small red flowers

calmly grow without us. He returns and helps me up,
the wounded dove cupped in his left hand,
throat pumping like a rusted piston.
My father raises her high above our heads

where her black eye spins skyward.
Even the most cautious love
can deliver you into violence.

In the Great Green Room

His truck rabbit-hole rolls,
down I go,
tree trunks rooted up
feet delicate and cloud carried
until it stops snug around a lamp post.
The liquor store's sign, kitty-corner from our crash,
blinks a neon treasure chest. Inside the chest
diamonds, booze, pearls flash.
Sideways, the Skyy
vodka in the blue-frosted bottle
still jarred between my father's legs,
waterfalls on my lap.
The engine ticks an unwound time.
It's late, late like I have never stayed up
so long past bedtime.
Streetlight falls in on the driver's side safely
in a way that makes me believe a story
will be pulled from beneath the seat,
Goodnight Moon, and somewhere out there
a comb, and a brush, and a bowl full of mush.

Now Every Man's Arm Is Fire

The dog is always with me,
sleek and late-hour black.
Even as dawn outlines
branches where silkworms weave
a veil, a net, a ladder to spring from,
I hear him breathing ash,
smelling like a burning doll house
and all the dolls inside, all burning.
Just beyond the hedges
he roots in the dirt,
searching for what's buried,
for what belongs to him.

Great Expectations

After drifting through unlit neighborhoods
for over an hour,
the Ativan, Methadone mix loops
the wrong way through my system
and I swear a dog has followed me from the party,

a black puppet stitched
into night's bleak backdrop.
The plan was to sleep
with a guy who seemed too careless to worry
about my face, the burn
like a brand, the scar like a damned scar.
But he ditched to get Taco Bell,
whose all-night drive-thru and manic fluorescence
left me wedged awkwardly
against the wall,

watching the party spin
and wind down like the music box
my Grandma gave me,
the one with a plastic ballerina that spun when I raised the lid,
pink box that Dad, Pop, Paw kicked against the wall,

the top snapping off, the twirling girl falling
down the air vent.
I've only lived here, in this new town
I thought would open like an orange at Christmas,
for a week. Only a week and already
the feeling of a world wholly dark, with every curb a ledge
to fall into the street.

The Money Shot

I'll shave everything in advance,
beginning with the delicate bend behind the knee
that feels like a sexual artery,
a tendon that could be cut
without much effort,
a pale patch that burns
after the first close shearing.

Next, the always loose older elbow,
so dry and unlady-like.
Every safety is sacrificed.
The way I must prop my leg up and bow
to reach with my three-bladed razor,
the pieces of myself I must pull over.

More animal than doll, like an ostrich
down in the dirt, a porcupine,
a loose-necked hen with her wattle
swinging about.
And then, I guess I should kneel
and let them own it.

I'll open my mouth, bare my begging uvula
so my guts coat with saliva, which they do
naturally when I'm going to vomit.
This is the acme, the moment
when all the men grab harder and push,
stretch their thick-veined necks
back and moan,
exposing their throbbing throats.

The Test

You took forever to open the door. I heard you inside, coming down the stairs, touching things, moving your slippered feet. You sounded older than I'd ever seen you. I held it, double lines and terrible, behind my back b/c I couldn't possibly imagine it anywhere else, anywhere in front or inside, already beating its little multi-celled heart. Already binding us, more than we were already bound. First, b/c we met in astronomy class, met, as they say, under the stars. You believed in thrown-out science, believed the universe was constant. Bound b/c both our brothers died early, and tragic. B/c our fathers were dead and missing and getting hit by cars somewhere across town. B/c we both knew someone we loved once lived in the Arrowhead Motel. We knew what that meant. You thought I was there to kill you; a knife behind my back. And I wonder, now, after, what you wished, *which was worse*. It was already oscillating inside my body, spinning purple green like the June bugs in the brown-leafed murk around your house. Inside your house was my body. Inside my body was a mood ring changing color. You did not love me, did not love yourself, did not love any street in Indiana or any bar we frequented. I faked every orgasm. I falsified every joy and I showed you the test and I did the usual crying and you carried me upstairs and we lay down on your bed and slept and slept and ate Chinese and you said we could keep it. I said we could keep it and we made plans the next day, kind of like a mini-vacation, to drive four hours to Cincinnati and finally put an end to that happiness. On the long drive there and the longest drive back you were silent. Just as you were silent when your father said God spoke to him, silent when that horse smashed your young brother's skull, the way a bullet blew through mine, silent when you came inside me. And after all that time, all that smashing together, spinning apart, I still couldn't believe you thought the universe was steady and unchanging as a river, as a body, as a cell.

Why We Bird

Nightjars fly to the junipers and pines,
more skins of bark,
loaned-out lungs unhinged
from our poor creaking cavity.
A fearless, unfamiliar song uncorks the forest—

                                        our exhale

without the bodily burden.
We are only the lookout. We can't support

                                the arctic tern over the sea
on her impossible polar journey,
                      but we love
that she's tireless and we praise
ourselves for making it through
the abortion and our brother's death.

A glossy ibis wades the freshwater—
our father's roaming, wasted life.

Silent thrum, a humming bird
pierces the plastic flowers
we draw around us like hope.
With stained necks,
as if someone slit their delicate throats,

                                they rise like ghosts.

They tell us our bones are hollow
and collapsible. They tell us

we will never die.
One in four people are birders. One in four

wait for a Great Bird to cast his shadow,
the way a distant cloud shades
a distant mountain
and we can see it's happening. We can see
outside the realm
               of dark, for once,
we are not under it.

The American

Dream about houses, all night
                    all night,

Dream about
thin drywall, plastered to frame like a hornet's nest

built by spit. A deep blue flood light
falls over an empty dilapidated pool.

Foundations unfasten and widen inch by inch
                    widen until a hand can reach in.

Radon rises from damp
radon in the well water
        the well water poisoned, drink
    from a well,   poisoned.

The lawn furniture rusts and stains the cushions.
The lawn
opens and swallows the garage,
                  the garage is tunneled with termites
ground bees and water damage,
                damage.

Dream about a high fence surrounding the property
with no gate in, no exit.

At the end of a brick walkway, a light
                left on, a light that calls
the creatures to its burning circle

*

littered with wounded civilians.
The alluring spotlight drags
the creatures and burns
                and burns out with barely any notice.

The Traveler

In the cypress, swallows
sleep and preen. Voices soft,

they churr in the knotted tree.
Each swallow is an individual

hymn, sung as branches bob
like metronomes beneath them.

I change soiled sheets and pray,
wash dishes and feed my father ice chips,

wading waist deep through the last hours
before morning.

He evaporates in the coming fog.
His mouth open, cracking like the dry banks,

is the mouth of a spirit fish.
He rattles.

Cumulus build into cathedrals,
thunder tolls, the swallows rise

and file past the windows.
He will not stop looking at me,

one eye swimming against the lid,
and I look out, past the cypress—

*

The way his body reflects,
against the window and the view

of the river beyond,
looks like a traveler adrift,

his bed a raft, his lamp a lantern
guiding the way downstream.

I Do Not Know You

But I know your face—
at birth I took it as my own.
I trace the lines around my mouth
and know the way you spoke
when angry, the only way
you ever spoke.

I remember your tattoos from Jamaica,
where they said you got hooked,
and as a child, I pictured only a fish,
blinking in disbelief at his life
outside of water.

No one bothered to tell me
where your ashes scattered.
So I can't picture rolling hills,
or a calm lake for you to float.
Your other family has taken everything
with care. Taken care of everything.

You picked me up for the weekend once,
driving your rust-eaten pickup,
beer between your legs,
Jimmy Buffet aching from the radio.
I rolled my window down
so everyone could see us together.

Scent

And though my father became a needle of blackbirds
stitched through sky, these inner folds
in last spring's linens are exactly the way he smelled.

From the valley of a drowsy Sunday,
a sunlit road reveals a tunnel of dust
and my cerebral attic swings

open. A door unlatches from the ceiling,
a door I didn't even know was there—

*

I would not dive without knowing
the water was deep enough,
would not dive even when he swore it was safe.
He pushed me in and I disappeared underneath

his reflection looming over the quarry.
The shale rock at the bottom cut deep,
as if my father sought to teach me
never to trust him.

*

I can't see the water
pipes turning in question marks
under these floorboards
any more than I can lead

*

with a dowsing rod or a branch
forking with truth and know
where the well should be struck
or where rivers run alluvial beneath us.

I don't know how to find
what I'm searching for,
where I should fall to my knees
and dig if I am thirsty.

After the Hunt

Here's the body the dogs robbed—
the limbs strewn around the field like prophecy.
She won't make it,
they say. They say
the body found in her bed
was eaten right through to the floral mattress.
They had to shut her eyes
because she would not stop
blinking up at a bone marrow-colored sky,
enjoying her party, the confetti
of her flayed body.
The dogs got sick on her form,
the remains of her last meal of steamed artichoke,
grapes, mercy, and rejection.
Don't they know
what's good for one
will poison another? So
they say. They say
the dogs died in a circle
and she rose the next day
to bury them and bring flowers
to their graves.

The Winter Following My Father's Death

The deer came dressed as bone
because snow, winter's best linen,
silently buried the food.
He lies on the concrete in the wildlife rescue
pumping straw-stalk legs.
I've thrown myself over him,
my ribs on his, two brittle cages,
while the vet shaves a patch of fur.
She tries to keep his rolling veins steady.
He is young, maybe his first frost
foraging without a mother, without antlers,
hauling an endless hunger.

Blood wells where the needle pulls.
Will a deer bruise, will it grieve
those painful colors?
I have to hold his head up or he will choke
when we try to tube feed.
His neck is so long and graceful
I know I would paint it stiff, stunted.
His neck, a wobbling
ballerina. And his barely-blinking
black eye is nowhere close
to here. It sees field,

the opening in the wood's break.
It is true that deer do not see red,
but their vision cuts through dark,
perceives a blue more brilliant than any
artist's mineral. This deer must know my face
as two cobalt burns, as moonlike.

*

My muscles fade into numbness,
it is just this deer I feel, our bodies
dredged from roadside
river ditches. The wildlife
always listening. And then
his nostrils puff no more invitations
and I don't even notice at first, his
death like I round a corner and
swerve into a stranger that says
he knows me
better than I know myself.

Even as We Sleep

                we know
something parts from us—
sailboat catching
                wind to grow small and vanish,
ripples   trailing in the dresser mirror,

reeds
      nodding in the brief waves.

    Island   selves
abandoned nightly,

                tide picking through
what to carry   out, what to offer
as housewarming—

garland shells and sea foam.
      We see ourselves pushing   off,
dark oars in hand. We tie the last

rope, that solid   mortal coil,
which connected us to the mainland,

        and pile it, gently, in the boat's dusty bottom.
We push off   we grow small and vanish,

reeds nodding in the brief waves.

Landfall

When I was small
I hid behind my body's many locks.
My dead father breaks through doors.
My dead brother sets the fires.
Boot marks busied my back,
forcing me to sleep stomach down. Downed wire shocked
heat into the ground I buried myself under.
                      I buried myself under

childhood's rusted hammer,
bludgeoned as a casualty and survivor.
The eternal past trains its cycloptic eye inland.
The eternal past

revolves inward. Driven up by surge,
as bodies sometimes resurrect
when water dips its little feet
into our soil-tossed cemeteries,
our lawn used to fill with shit, used condoms, and tampons.
Filthy, we stood on the front porch
unable to leave unless we waded.
Ringworm's beauty mark
shamed me with its wandering itch.
The whole house, surrendered to rot run riot.
                      Surrendered to

roaches and blind-drinking when the power was cut.
The pale-mouthed possum, the childhood mother,
unrolls her pink tongue. She tries to kill herself still,
the pill bottle bottomless, the notes

her half-gone hand formed
come through waiflike static,
an ethereal hiss—remember.
						Remember

in those early days it rained upward, as if I'm recalling
earth's volatile birth, violent tectonics,
vapor, devastating comets,
all in a mute providence to form something livable someday.
But sometimes it's hard enduring, isn't it,
	sometimes it's hard

to keep separate the life which delivered me,
miraculously, to adulthood's wide sheltered streets of silver and oak.
The staggering trunk of the neighbor's tree
never waivers. I am in my future, I will not fall though.
			In my future,

no one strikes me, no swirling metal chain
busts my teeth, wind, the words, from my mouth,
no one smokes crystal,
the lighted pipe's color crackling
like an oil slick rainbow. All the dangerous shadows
barely dance along the wall.
Those that tried to shoot me are dead now; at last, I can love them
from a safe distance.

ACKNOWLEDGMENTS

First and always, I want to thank my brother, Chris, for existing in the world, if only for a short time. I don't really want to thank my father, but I wouldn't be here without him. I also thank my mother. Thank you taking me to the library, and exposing me to the greatest love of my life—books.

I also want to thank Jim McGarrah, Ron Mitchell, and Matthew Graham, my first creative writing professors and mentors who gave me every chance and opportunity to succeed. I wouldn't have made it here without your guidance and support.

And I don't believe in soul mates, but if I did, it would be A.M. Brant. Thank you for being my sounding board in poetry and in life. I couldn't manage without you.

Another big thanks to the Hollins Faculty and especially to Thorpe Moeckel who challenged my ideas of sound and imagery and led me through many early versions of these poems.

Thank you to my partner, Justin, for putting up with my rigorous schedules, my constant anxiety, and my bottomless need for control and validation.

Lastly, I want to thank New American Press for choosing my manuscript. Thank you David Bowen for all your kind attention and hard work on this project. I also want to thank the late Okla Elliott, a beautiful and kind person who made this book, and many others, possible. He was such a gift to the literary community.

BRITTNEY SCOTT received an MFA from Hollins University in Roanoke, Virginia. Her poems appear online and in print in a variety of journals and anthologies, including the inaugural anthology of *Bettering American Poetry 2015*. A finalist in the 2013 *Narrative* 30 Below Contest, she is also the 2012 recipient of the Joy Hargo Prize for Poetry and the Dorothy Sargent Rosenberg Poetry Prize. She is an assistant professor of English at John Tyler Community College. She homesteads on seven acres in rural Virginia.

www.ingramcontent.com/pod-product-compliance
Lightning Source LLC
LaVergne TN
LVHW041340080426
835512LV00006B/549